HANUKKAH AT VALLEY FORGE

STEPHEN KRENSKY — illustrated by GREG HARLIN

Hanukkah
· AT ·
Valley Forge

The paintings were created with transparent and opaque watercolors
on cold-press watercolor paper.

Apples & Honey Press
An Imprint of Behrman House Publishers
Millburn, New Jersey 07041
www.applesandhoneypress.com

ISBN 978-1-68115-584-5

Text copyright © 2006, 2021 by Stephen Krensky
Illustrations copyright © 2006 by Greg Harlin

Originally published in 2006 by Dutton Children's Books.
Revised edition published in 2021 by Apples & Honey Press.

Library of Congress Control Number: 2021930784

Printed in China

1 3 5 7 9 8 6 4 2

For Tamar Mays and Steve Meltzer
—SK

*To my daughter, Hannah, and to all
future caretakers of history*
—GH

EDITOR'S NOTE: Special thanks to Dr. Lee Levine, professor of Jewish history and archaeology at the Hebrew University in Israel, and Rabbi Scott Weiner of the Hebrew Tabernacle Synagogue in New York, for their invaluable help in recreating the ancient Temple.

The general stood tall on a ridge at Valley Forge, surveying his troops below. The December night was clear, but the wind cut cruelly through his heavy coat. The general shook his head, shrugging the cold aside.

It was his soldiers he was worried about.

For more than two years his army had been at war. The general had not expected the fighting to be easy. War was never easy. But some of his soldiers lacked weapons to defend themselves. Others were without coats or shoes. And nobody had enough to eat.

"An army of skeletons," one witness had called them.

The snow crunched dryly under the general's boots as he walked through the camp. In one crude hut, a young soldier was sitting at a small table.

The general watched from the doorway as the soldier lit a candle. He was speaking softly, so softly that the general could not catch his words.

The general cleared his throat. "A cold night, is it not?" he said.

The startled soldier jumped up. "General Washington!" he cried.

The soldier swallowed nervously. "It was colder than this," he said finally, "when I was a boy in Poland. But even then my family would always light candles for *Hanukkah.*"

"Hanukkah?" the general repeated. The word was unfamiliar to him.

"The name for a celebration. I was just finishing a prayer in Hebrew, sir, in honor of what once happened."

"Ah, then you are of the children of Abraham." The general's gaze was intent. "Tell me more of *Hanukkah*."

"Over two thousand years ago," the soldier began, "my people, the people of Israel, were ruled by Antiochus, a Greek king from far away. He did not allow them to pray to their God and follow their customs. He wanted them to worship his gods, the Greek gods."

General Washington nodded. "The fight for liberty is an ancient one. And no one likes squirming under the thumb of a distant king."

The soldier looked at his candle. "In my homeland, our family could not follow our beliefs either, except in secret. That is why I came to America."

"But the people of Israel were not so fortunate. In a village near Jerusalem, the Greek soldiers ordered them to bow to idols. Among the Israelites, a high priest named Mattathias refused to obey and angrily drew his sword. In the fight that followed, Mattathias escaped.

"He and his five sons, the Maccabees, became the leaders of a rebellion. Some said they were foolish, that they were risking their lives in a doomed cause. But the Maccabees fought on. Their force was small, but they did not give up."

The general sighed. Independence from England had been declared eighteen months earlier, in July 1776. But he too was mired in an uphill fight.

"I understand," he said. "We also face a cruel enemy who leaves us only with the choice of brave resistance or abject submission."

"There was one battle," the soldier went on, "where the army of the Maccabees was greatly outnumbered.

"But Mattathias's son Judah rallied their troops. He reminded them that battles were not won or lost solely on strength in the field. 'For our enemies trust in arms and acts of daring,' said Judah, 'but we trust in the Almighty God.'

"Judah and his army won that fight, but many more followed. After three years, though, the Maccabees finally drove their enemies from their land."

"The Israelites rejoiced in their freedom and set about cleaning the Temple. But when it came time to light the Temple menorah, they could only find enough oil for one day. That was troubling. Once lit, this menorah was never supposed to go out. Still, they did not want to wait any longer to open the Temple. So they lit the menorah, trusting that God would somehow help them find more oil."

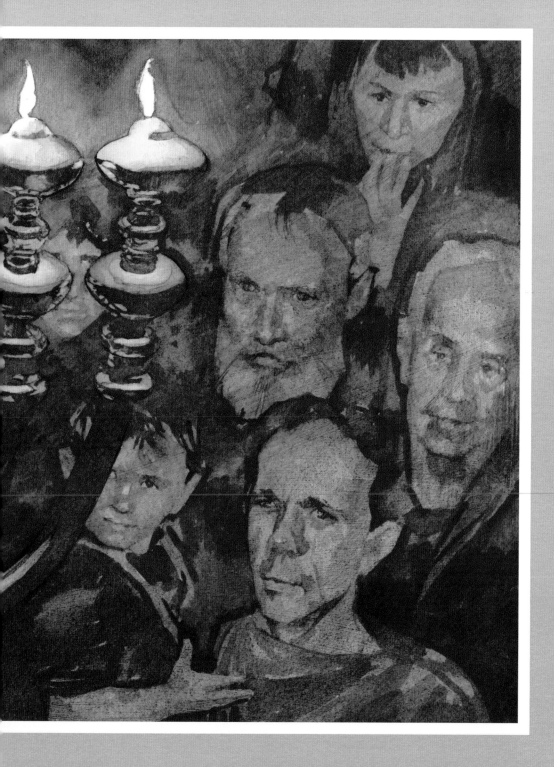

"One day passed quickly, and no oil was found. Yet the light remained strong. Another day went by. Still there was no oil, but the flames did not dim. Three days, four days, the hunt continued. But all the fighting and destruction made finding oil very difficult. In all, eight days passed before any new oil arrived.

"And in all that time, the lights of the menorah never went out."

The soldier blew on his hands to warm them. "Truly a miracle happened there. So every year we remember this festival of lights. Tonight is the first night of Hanukkah, and therefore I lit only the first candle of the Hanukkah menorah. I will use this special candle, the *shamash*, to light one more candle each night until there are eight. Eight candles to honor the eight days that the oil lasted."

The general made ready to leave. "Your tale is a brave one. And your candle has brightened my evening. Perhaps we are not as lost as our enemies would have us believe. I rejoice in the Maccabees' success, though it is long past." He smiled grimly. "And it pleases me to think that miracles may still be possible."

The soldier nodded. "The world would be a poor place without them."

"So it would," said General Washington, with a lighter mood than he had felt in many a day. As he continued on his rounds, the winds quieted, and the Hanukkah candles burned long into the night.